D0458521

GAUGUIN
BY
Gauguin.

Breton Girl Seated, 1886, Musée des Arts Africains et Oceaniens, Paris

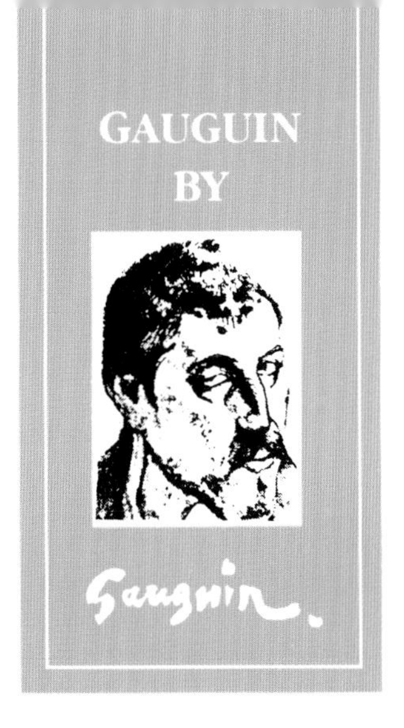

ARTISTS BY THEMSELVES

EDITED AND WITH AN INTRODUCTION

BY RACHEL BARNES

BRACKEN
BOOKS

Series devised by Nicky Bird

This edition published 1992 by The Promotional Reprint Company Limited exclusively for Bracken Books, an imprint of Studio Editions Limited, Princess House, 50 Eastcastle Street, London W1N 7AP England.

ISBN 1 85170 979 7

CONTENTS

INTRODUCTION

> For I am an artist and you are right, you are not mad. I am a great artist and I know it. It is because I am such that I have endured such sufferings. To do what I have done in any other circumstances would make me out as a ruffian. Which I am no doubt for many people. Anyhow, what does it matter? What distresses me most is not so much the poverty as the perpetual obstacles to my art, which I cannot practise as I feel ought to be done and as I could do it if relieved of the poverty which ties my hands.

Paul Gauguin wrote these words in a letter to his estranged wife, Mette, after he had rejected the civilization of Paris in favour of the primitive island of Tahiti and the life of 'the noble savage'.

In order to pursue his artistic vision, Gauguin had by this stage already given up a successful career as a stockbroker in Paris, together with the bourgeois comforts that accompanied such a life; permanently abandoned his wife and their five children; and himself endured several years of poverty and hardship. His vocation to paint was to cause him continued problems and suffering until his lonely death in 1903 on the remote island of Hivaoa, but he made these sacrifices willingly – not only for himself, but also for a number of others, not least his own family.

Along with fellow Post-Impressionists Van Gogh and Cézanne, Gauguin was responsible for changing the rôle of the artist in Western society. Personal suffering and isolation seemed a necessary part of achieving artistic fulfilment – the Christ analogy was one

Self-Portrait Dedicated to Carriere, 1888-95, National Gallery of Art, Washington; Collection of Mr and Mrs Paul Mellon

which Gauguin used frequently, even painting his own features for the crucified Christ on the cross. The importance of this evolution of the artist's rôle cannot be underestimated, and it continues to affect us today. 'The public owes me nothing since my work is only relatively good, but the painters of today who profit from this liberty owe me something,' Gauguin wrote prophetically.

The life of Paul Gauguin, which has sometimes attracted more attention than his art, is frequently presented as the extraordinary crisis of a man in his middle years who suddenly decides that everything he has previously held dear – family, career and material success – is to be sacrificed in favour of the perilous life of an artist. This is held to be even more extraordinary in that he had only the flimsiest indication from the outside world as to the existence of his talent. Certainly his Danish wife could hardly have had less premonition of this sudden and appalling turn of events when she married him in 1873, as her husband had entirely neglected to inform her of his interest in art. He was, in fact, already painting when he met her, and by the following year had begun his important friendship with Camille Pissarro, who encouraged him and influenced his early Impressionist years.

Gauguin was born in Paris in 1848, the son of a radical political journalist. It is interesting to note that writing genes were in the blood on both sides of the family: his maternal grandmother, Flora Tristan, was a pioneering feminist who had published both a novel and her memoirs.

The normality of Gauguin's earliest childhood was interrupted by Napoleon's *coup d'état*, which prompted the family to embark for Peru where Paul's mother, Aline Chazal, had relatives. On the journey out, however, the family suffered the trauma of the sudden death of Gauguin's father. Aline made the decision to stay in Peru

Garden under Snow, 1879, NY Carlsberg Glyptotek, Copenhagen

with her children for the next few years and it was here, in early childhood, that Gauguin acquired his passion for exotic landscape. Returning to Paris at the age of twelve, Europe must have seemed visually dull and uninspiring after the tropical splendours of South America. As soon as he could, at the age of seventeen, he escaped to visit warmer climes with the merchant navy.

In retrospect, given Gauguin's maverick, iconoclastic and often arrogant personality, the next years, when he married an ordinary bourgeois girl and settled down to his stockbroker career, are more of a mystery than his later rebellion and subsequent peregrinations. Yet even in these early years, his desire to paint was forming.

Mette was understandably shattered and bewildered when her husband revealed his decision to embark on a career as a painter, and never forgave him for abandoning her and their children. Their subsequent communications reveal great chasms of bitterness on both sides, as quotations in this book will show. He, in turn, never forgave her for her uncompromising and unforgiving response, in particular when it affected his relationships with his children, whom he continued to love and care for despite his defection. It was no coincidence that his suicide attempt in 1897 in Tahiti followed shortly after the death of his favourite child, Aline, for whom he had written *Cahier pour Aline*.

Gauguin's bold, Synthetiste style had, in fact, evolved before he embarked on his voyage to Tahiti. His earliest years had been dominated by the influence of Impressionism, most especially the flat areas of colour used by Cézanne and the complicated perspective of Degas. But in 1886 he decided to make a move to Brittany, attracted by his interest in the ancient traditions and folklore of this comparatively unspoiled region of France, together with reports of the low cost of living. It was here that Gauguin developed his friendship with the young artist, Emile Bernard. The latter's painting 'Breton Women in a Meadow', with its strong, dark outlines influenced by the Japanese print and its complete absence of modelling, was to have a seminal effect on Gauguin's change of style in favour of the bold juxtaposition of primary colours and the high symbolic content which characterizes his later years. Together, Bernard and Gauguin developed a style which became known as 'cloissonisme', since it originally derived from the cloissonné enamel, with its strong colours separated by black lead lines.

Vahine no te Tiare, (Tahitian with a Flower), 1891, NY Carlsberg Glyptotek, Copenhagen

Influenced by Bernard's interest in religion, and turning his back on Impressionist secularism, many of Gauguin's themes in this period are biblical, if not conventionally religious. Later he wrote:

> Brittany has made me a Catholic ready to fight for the Church . . . I became intoxicated with incense, with organ music, stained glass, hieratic tapestries. Little by little, I became a man of the Middle Ages.

This statement, however, does not fully convey his rebellious and frequently tendentious images of Christianity which, even today, might be regarded as blasphemous.

At this time, Gauguin began to project his artistic personality both through his writing and through such paintings as 'Good Morning, Monsieur Gauguin' (see p35). This image of the wandering, restless spirit at odds with both himself and society was one which stuck, perhaps because it was, indeed, largely based on the truth. Gauguin's notion of styling himself as an artistic celebrity, a legend in his own lifetime, was supposed to have derived, at least in part, from the fame-seeking American James McNeill Whistler.

As a painter interested in a wide variety of different visual sources, both ethnic and classical, Gauguin was highly eclectic. Before he embarked on his first voyage to Tahiti in 1891 he was already drawing freely from folk art, caricature, medieval sculpture, stained glass, Japanese prints, Persian manuscripts and Far Eastern sculpture. Later, in Tahiti, he discovered the primitive arts of the South Sea Islands, which were to provide him with a further source of inspiration. Although he frequently asserted that everything in art had gone wrong with the Greeks, this did not prevent him from borrowing freely from the Parthenon frieze in works such as 'The Calf'. In 'Ta Matete' (see p53) there is more than a hint of the stiff, posed bearing found in Egyptian wall painting.

Gauguin's stay in Brittany was broken in October 1888 by his long-planned trip to join Vincent Van Gogh in Arles – Theo Van Gogh had helped to arrange this much needed company for his brother. Gauguin's complete break with Impressionism and his tendency to use increasingly stylized form was evident in the self portrait he sent to Vincent before the visit. His growing preoccupation with literary ideas and with Symbolism was expressed in his reference to Victor Hugo's novel *Les Misérables*. He wrote of the painting to his friend Emile Schuffenecker:

> I made a portrait of myself for Vincent, who asked me for it. I think it's one of my best things: so abstract that it's absolutely incomprehensible (I suppose). A bandit's head at first sight, a Jean Valjean (*Les Misérables*) also personifying an Impressionist painter, run down and bearing the chains of the world. Its drawing is very special (complete abstraction). Eyes, mouth and nose are like flowers of Persian carpets which also embody the symbolic aspect. The colour is rather far from nature: it reminds you vaguely of my pottery gone lopsided because of a hot kiln.

Te Reroia, 1897, Courtauld Institute Galleries, London. Courtauld Collection

The plan for Gauguin to join Vincent in the South of France was a response to Vincent's highly romantic idyll of a 'studio in the South', where like-minded artists should live and work together, exchanging ideas in a happy and creative atmosphere. Gauguin and Vincent were both isolated and extremely hard up, and the idea of sharing expenses as well as artistic ideas seemed a good one. Sadly, the polemically different characters of the two men were to result in a personality clash that ended in tragic consequences.

At first, everything seemed to go well. Vincent had been in a fever of preparation for weeks, getting everything in the little yellow house ready, pathetically anxious that Gauguin should approve of his set up. This humility and lack of confidence on Vincent's part were traits which the arrogant Gauguin was to find incomprehensible. The two men soon started to have discussions which all too often turned into verbally violent arguments. One of the major topics of these bitter disputes was the rôle of reality and the outside world in art. At the time, Gauguin summed up their paradoxical natures in a letter:

> He admires Daumier, Daubigny, Ziem and the great Rousseau whom I cannot stand. And on the other hand he detests Ingres, Raphael, Degas and all those whom I admire... He is romantic, while I am more inclined towards a primitive state. As to colour he is interested in the accidents of thickly applied paint, as with Monticelli, where I detest the worked out surface.

There is little evidence of any mutual exchange of artistic influence between the two men at this stage, although these heated discussions probably helped them to confirm and consolidate the direction each was taking.

Unfortunately, this was not the only consequence of the arguments. Clearly Gauguin lacked either the sensitivity, or possibly the compassion, to observe that these rows were having a terrible effect on the already nervous and excitable Vincent. Quite possibly, he had been heading for a breakdown for some time, whilst his hereditary mental illness still lay dormant. The terrible climax to this build-up of tension between the two men ended in the famous incident of Vincent severing his ear lobe and sending it to a girl in the local brothel.

Gauguin has often been held at least partially to blame for the part he played in the onset of Vincent's illness, which was to lead to his desperate suicide two years later. Certainly, he appeared to behave in a somewhat callous and selfish way, which was not entirely untypical, although there are indications in letters he wrote later that he did care about the mental collapse of his friend, but felt powerless to help him. In the last year of his life in Tahiti, 1903,

Are You Jealous? Hermitage, Leningrad

he was still brooding about it all and wrote in his account *Avant et Après:*

> In *Les Monstres* Jean Dolent writes:
> 'When Gauguin says "Vincent," his voice is gentle'.
> Without knowing it, but having guessed it, Jean Dolent is right.
> One knows why . . .

The two trips to Tahiti, the first from 1891-3 and the next in 1895, provided the material for the fulfilment of Gauguin's artistic vision. He had often boasted of what he called his 'half-savage temperament', and had for some time felt a very genuine desire to escape the industrial and materialistic society in Europe. Contemporary painters were, on the whole, completely baffled by this. 'But one paints so well at Batignolles', was Renoir's comment on hearing of Gauguin's intrepid plans.

Although the Tahitian years were marked by terrible poverty and hardship, at least by European standards, and frequent disillusionment with the reality of life in comparison with the romantic idyll he had held of a tropical paradise, it was arguably in these last years that Gauguin painted his best work. In his book *Noa Noa,* begun in 1893 during his first trip to Tahiti, Gauguin describes in vivid detail how he adopted the life of a noble savage, taking a thirteen-year-old girl, Tehura, as his concubine, eating the local fish and roots, and adopting the native dress of a sarong. Gauguin's literary style in *Noa Noa,* quoted extensively in this book, is deliberately modern, a stream of consciousness, and carefully creates and promotes his own legend. Despite this tendency to self-consciousness, the painter's own colourful descriptions of life on the

Studies of Horses, Museum Boymans-van Beuningen, Rotterdam

island and of its inhabitants provide the reader with a fascinating and illuminating background to the extraordinary paintings he produced at this time. Unlike many of his contemporaries, Gauguin, as has already been indicated, was by no means averse to revealing other aspects of his artistic identity through his writing. It is especially helpful to a deeper understanding of his paintings to see these thoughts juxtaposed on the following pages with the works in question.

Self Portrait

1885

Private Collection, Bern
Photograph: Hans Hinz

For I am an artist and you are right, you are not mad, I am a great artist and I know it. It is because I am such that I have endured such sufferings. To do what I have done in any other circumstances would make me out as a ruffian. Which I am no doubt for many people. Anyhow, what does it matter? What distresses me most is not so much the poverty as the perpetual obstacles to my art, which I cannot practise as I feel it ought to be done and as I could do it if relieved of the poverty which ties my hands. You tell me that I am wrong to remain far away from the artistic centre. No, I am right, I have known for a long time what I am doing, and why I do it. My artistic centre is in my brain and not elsewhere and I am strong because I am never sidetracked by others, and do what is in me.

. . . No, I have an aim and I am always pursuing it, building up material. There are transformations every year, it is true, but they always follow each other in the same direction. I alone am logical. Consequently, I find very few who follow me for long.

Poor Schuffenecker, who reproaches me for being wholehearted in my volitions! But if I did not behave in this manner, could I have endured the endless struggle I am waging for one year? My actions, my painting, etc, are criticized and repudiated every time, but in the end I am acknowledged to be right. I am always starting all over again. I believe I am doing my duty, and strong in this, I accept no advice and take no blame. The conditions in which I am working are unfavourable, and one must be a colossus to do what I am doing in these circumstances...

Letter to Mette Gauguin, March 1892

The Painter's Family in the Garden, Rue Carcel

1882

Ny Carlsberg Glyptotek, Copenhagen

At the moment, I'm at the end of my courage and resources. Misery in a foreign town! No credit and no money; each day I wonder if it wouldn't be better to go to the attic and put a rope around my neck. What holds me back is painting; this is my stumbling block. Wife, family, everybody, hangs this cursed painting over me, claiming that it's a shame not to earn one's living. But a man's capacities cannot satisfy two things and I *can only do one thing*: paint. I'm terrible at everything else. To paint, I don't have anything to buy colours with, so I've limited myself to drawing – it's less expensive. The German colours sold here are awful; they don't dry easily and after a while, some places are still oily while others are completely dry. And I can't sell anything – neither a drawing nor a painting, not even for ten francs. In a short time, I will send a few things to Paris; ask Durand-Ruel to take something *at any price* so that I can buy some colours...

Letter to Camille Pissarro, May 1885

Mette Gauguin in Evening Dress

1884

Nasjonalgalleriet, Oslo

Photograph: Jacques Lathion

Yes, you have not heard from me for over six months; but it is more than six months since I received news of the children. It seems there must be a serious accident before I do hear, which scarcely disposes me to cheerfulness, although you say all danger is now over.

What is it you want of me? Above all, what you have ever wanted of me? Whether in the Indies or elsewhere, I am, it appears, to be a beast of *burden* for wife and children whom I *must not see*. By way of return for my homeless existence, I am *to be loved if I love,* I am to be *written to if* I write. You know me. Either I weigh matters (and weigh them well) or I do not. Heart in hand, eyes front, and I fight with uncovered breast.

. . . I determined, despite the certitude which my conscience gave me, to consult others (men who also count) to ascertain if I was doing my duty. All are of my opinion, that art is my business, my capital, the future of my children, the honour of the name I have given them – all things which will be useful to them one day. When they have to make their way in the world, a famous father may prove a valuable asset.

You will retort that this will be a long time ahead, but what do you want me to do about it? Is it my fault? I am the first to suffer from it. I can assure you that if those who know about such things had said that I have no talent and that I am wasting my time, I would have abandoned the attempt long ago. Can it be said that Millet failed in his duty and bequeathed a wretched future to his children?

Letter to Mette Gauguin, 1889

[23]

Tropical Vegetation

1887

National Gallery of Scotland, Edinburgh

I'm writing to you this time from Martinique – I'd planned on coming here much later. Bad luck has been against me for a long time, and I don't do what I want. I had been working for two weeks for the Société when orders from Paris came to suspend much of the work, and the same day ninety employees were fired, and so on; naturally, I was listed as a newcomer. I took my trunks, and I came here. It's not a bad thing; Laval had just come down with a bout of yellow fever that I eased with homeopathy. Anyway, all's well that ends well.

For the time being, both of us are living in a Negroes' cabin, and it's a paradise near the isthmus. Below us, the sea bordered by coconut trees, overhead every sort of fruit tree, twenty-five minutes from town. Negro men and women walk by all day long with their Creole songs and endless chattering; not that it's monotonous, on the contrary it's quite varied. I couldn't describe for you my enthusiasm for life in the *French* colonies, and I'm sure that you'd feel the same. Nature at its richest, a hot climate, but with intermittent cool spells. With only a little money, there's enough to be happy. But one does need a certain amount. Thus, today with *30,000 francs*, you could buy property that would bring in a yearly income of 8,000 to 10,000 francs and live off of it as well, that is, eat like a gourmand.

Letter to Mette Gauguin, June 1887

Van Gogh Painting Sunflowers

1888

Vincent Van Gogh Foundation, Vincent Van Gogh Museum, Amsterdam

For a long time I have wished to write about Van Gogh . . .

It is surely chance that in the course of my existence several men who have spent time in my company and with whom I've enjoyed discussions have gone mad. This was the case with the two Van Gogh brothers, and some, from evil intentions, and others, from naïveté, have attributed their madness to my doing. Certainly, some people may have more or less of an influence over their friends, but that is a far cry from provoking madness . . .

. . . The last letter that I had from him [Vincent] was dated Auvers, near Pontoise. He told me that he had hoped to recover enough to come to visit me in Brittany, but that now he was obliged to recognize the impossibility of a cure.

'Dear master (the only time that he had used this word), after having known you and caused you pain, it is more dignified to die in a good state of mind than in a degraded state.'

And he put a pistol shot in his stomach, and it was not until a few hours later, lying in his bed and smoking his pipe, that he died having complete lucidity of mind, with love for his art, and without hatred for others.

In *Les Monstres,* Jean Dolent writes:

'When Gauguin says "Vincent," his voice is gentle.'

Without knowing it, but having guessed it, Jean Dolent is right.

One knows why . . .

Extract from *Avant et Après,* 1903

Vision after the Sermon

1888

National Gallery of Scotland, Edinburgh

I just did a religious painting, very poorly done, but which was interesting to do and which pleases me. I wanted to give it to the church at Pont-Aven. Naturally, they don't want it.

Groups of Brittany women pray, very intense black costumes. Very bright yellow-white headdresses. The two headdresses on the right are like monstrous helmets. A dark purple apple tree crosses through the painting, with foliage drawn in masses like emerald green clouds with intervals of yellow-green sunlight. The (pure vermilion) land. At the church it slopes down and becomes red-brown.

The angel is dressed in violent ultramarine blue and Jacob bottle-green. The angel's wings of pure chromium yellow one. The angel's hair chromium two and orange flesh-coloured feet. I think I've succeeded in creating a great rustic and *superstitious* simplicity in the faces. The whole thing very severe. The cow under the tree is very small compared to life and rears up. In this painting I find that the landscape and the fight exist only in the imagination of the people who pray after the sermon – that's why there is a contrast between the life-sized people and the unnatural and disproportionate fight in its landscape.

Letter to Vincent Van Gogh, September 1888

Breton Calvary or The Green Christ

1888

Musée Royaux des Beaux-Arts de Belgique, Brussels
Photograph: G. Cussac

You speak to me of my *formidable* mysticism. Be an Impressionist to the end and do not be frightened of anything. Obviously, this Symbolist road is full of pitfalls and I have only just taken the first step, but it is in the depths of my nature and one must always follow his temperament. I well know that people will understand me *less and less*. What does it matter if I distance myself from others? For most I will be a puzzle, for a few I will be a poet, and sooner or later what's good will earn its place – no matter what, I tell you, I will end up doing things of *the first order*; I feel it and we will see. You well know that in art I am always right in the end. Be aware that right now there is a current among *the artists* that is highly favourable *to me*; I know of it because of certain indiscretions; don't worry, as much as Van Gogh loves me, he would not undertake to feed me in the Midi for my beautiful eyes. He studied the lay of the land like a cool Dutchman and intends to push things as much as possible, exclusively. I asked him to lower the prices to attract buyers. He replied that he intended, on the contrary, to raise them. Always the optimist, this time I am certainly walking on solid ground...

Letter to Emile Schuffenecker, October 1888

Self Portrait; Les Misérables

1888

Vincent Van Gogh Foundation, Vincent Van Gogh Museum, Amsterdam

I made a portrait of myself for Vincent, who asked me for it. I think it's one of my best things; so abstract that it's absolutely incomprehensible (I suppose). A bandit's head at first sight, a Jean Valjean (*Les Misérables*) also personifying an Impressionist painter, run down and bearing the chains of the world. Its drawing is very special (complete abstraction). Eyes, mouth, and nose are like flowers of Persian carpets which also embody the symbolic aspect. The colour is rather far from nature; it reminds you vaguely of my pottery gone lopsided because of a hot kiln. All the reds, the violets slashed through with fiery sparks, like a furnace shining in the eyes, the seat of the painter's struggling thoughts – everything on a pure chromium background sprinkled with childish bouquets – pure little girl's room.

Letter to Emile Schuffenecker, October 1888

les misérables
Vincent
P Gauguin 88

Good Morning, Monsieur Gauguin

1889

National Gallery, Prague

I am in a fisherman's inn at the seaside, near a village of 150 inhabitants. I live here like a peasant, and work every day in canvas trousers (all those of five years ago are worn out). I spend a franc a day on my food and two pence on tobacco. So no one can say I am extravagant. I speak to nobody, and I have no news of the children. Only – only this – I am exhibiting my works at Goupil's in Paris, and they are creating a great sensation; but it is difficult to sell them. When this is going to happen, I cannot tell you, but what I can tell you is that today I am one of the artists who arouse the greatest astonishment. You have exhibited some old things of mine at Copenhagen. My opinion might have been sought first of all.

Letter to Mette Gauguin, Le Pouldu, 1889

Self Portrait in Caricature

1889

National Gallery of Art, Washington DC; Chester Dale Collection

I think I said (in telegraph-style) what I wanted to say, perhaps with bitterness – you have to admit that there is reason – but from the depths of my heart and without any misunderstanding with you. You know that I have an Indian – Inca – background, and everything I do is affected by it. It is the depth of my personality. To rotten civilization, I aim to oppose something more natural, beginning with savageness. I would need a lot of time and ink to explain my painting to you, but I hope, however, that you will feel its uncertainty with this letter.

Letter to Theo Van Gogh, November 1889

889.

The Yellow Christ

1889

Albright-Knox Art Gallery, Buffalo, New York

On this matter, I'm quite sad to be held here in Pont-Aven; each day my debts increase and make my trip more and more unlikely. What a long calvary an artist's life is! And that's perhaps what makes us go on living. Passion gives life, and we die when it's no longer nourishing. Let's abandon these paths lined with thorny bushes, although they have their savage poetry...

Letter to Vincent Van Gogh, 1888

P Gauguin 89

Ave Maria

1891

The Metropolitan Museum of Art, New York

Bequest of Sam A. Lewisohn, 1951

I saw in this queen, already somewhat mature in years, only a commonplace stout woman with traces of noble beauty. When I saw her again later, I revised my first judgement. I fell under the spell of her 'Maori charm'. Notwithstanding all the intermixture, the Tahitian type was still very pure in her. And then the memory of her ancestor, the great chief Tati, gave her as well as her brother and all her family an appearance of truly imposing grandeur. She had the majestic sculptural form of her race, ample and at the same time gracious. The arms were like the two columns of a temple, simple, straight; and the whole bodily form with the long horizontal line of the shoulder, and the vast height terminating above in a point, inevitably made me think of the Triangle of the Trinity.

Extract from *Noa Noa*
1893-5

IA ORANA MARIA

The Loss of Virginity

1891

The Chrysler Museum, Norfolk, VA

You ask me, or rather you tell me, that people do not at all understand the work I do in wood. It is, however, simple. There is a nude of a woman, a man, a fox, and an inscription. Is that all!

Since you want literature, I am going to give you some (for you only).

At the top the rotting city of Babylon. At the bottom, as though through a window, a view of fields, nature with its flowers. Simple woman, whom a demon takes by the hand, who struggles despite the good advice of the tempting inscription. A fox (symbol of perversity among Indians). Several figures in this entourage who express the opposite of the advice 'you will be happy'), to show that it is fallacious. For those who want literature, there it is. But it is not for examination. The background of all this is sculptural art of *bas relief* forms and colours in the expression of the material. Between *the possible and the impossible*. The same for the painting of the three women of stone holding Christ.

Brittany, simple superstition and desolation.

The hill is guarded by a line of cows arranged up the hill. My intention in this painting is that everything should breathe passive belief, suffering, primitive religious style, and great nature with its cry.

Letter to Theo Van Gogh, November, 1889

Reverie

1891

The Nelson-Atkins Museum of Art, Kansas City, Missouri (Nelson Fund)

As I left the quay, at the moment of going on board, I saw Tehura for the last time.

She had wept through many nights. Now she sat worn-out and sad, but calm, on a stone with her legs hanging down and her strong, little feet touching the soiled water.

The flower which she had put behind the ear in the morning had fallen wilted upon her knee.

Here and there were others like her, tired, silent, gloomy, watching without a thought the thick smoke of the ship which was bearing all of us – lovers of a day – far away, forever.

From the bridge of the ship as we were moving farther and farther away, it seemed to us that with the telescope we could still read on their lips these ancient Maori verses:

Ye gentle breezes of the south and east
That join in tender play above my head,
Hasten to the neighbouring isle.
There you will find in the shadow of his favourite tree,
Him who has abandoned me.
Tell him that you have seen me weep.

Extract from *Noa Noa*
1893-5

Tahitian Landscape

1893

Hermitage, Leningrad

Several hours later dawn appeared, and we gently approached the reefs, entered the channel, and anchored without accidents in the roadstead.

The first view of this part of the island discloses nothing very extraordinary; nothing, for instance, that could be compared with the magnificent bay of Rio de Janeiro.

It is the summit of a mountain submerged at the time of one of the ancient deluges. Only the very point rose above the waters. A family fled thither and founded a new race – and then the corals climbed up along it, surrounding the peak, and in the course of centuries built a new land. It is still extending, but retains its original character of solitude and isolation, which is only accentuated by the immense expanse of the ocean.

Toward ten o'clock I made my formal call on the governor, the negro Lacascade, who received me as though I had been an important personage.

Extract from *Noa Noa,* 1893-5

When Will You Marry?

1892

Rudolf Staechelin Family Foundation, Basel
Photograph: Hans Hinz

As they were to me, so was I to them, an object for observation, a cause of astonishment – one to whom everything was new, one who was ignorant of everything. For I knew neither their language, nor their customs, not even the simplest, most necessary manipulations. As each one of them was a savage to me, so was I a savage to each one of them.

And which of us two was wrong?

Extract from *Noa Noa*
1893-5

NAFEA

Woman with a Mango

1892

The Baltimore Museum of Art: The Cone Collection,
formed by Dr Claribel Cone and Miss Etta Cone of Baltimore, Maryland

In order to familiarize myself with the distinctive characteristics of the Tahitian face, I had wished for a long time to make a portrait of one of my neighbours, a young woman of pure Tahitian extraction.

One day she finally became emboldened enough to enter my hut, and to look at photographs of paintings which I had hung on one of the walls of my room. She regarded the 'Olympia' for a long time and with special interest.

'What do you think of her?' I asked. I had learned a few Tahitian words during the two months since I had last spoken French.

My neighbour replied, 'She is very beautiful!'

. . . Without delay I began work, without hesitation and all of a fever. I was aware that on my skill as a painter would depend the physical and moral possession of the model, that it would be like an implied, urgent, irresistible invitation.

She was not at all handsome according to our aesthetic rules. She was beautiful. All her traits combined in a Raphaelesque harmony by the meeting of curves. Her mouth had been modelled by a sculptor who knew how to put into a single mobile line a mingling of all joy and all suffering.

I worked in haste and passionately, for I knew that the consent had not yet been definitely gained. I trembled to read certain things in these large eyes – fear and the desire for the unknown, the melancholy of bitter experience which lies at the root of all pleasure.

Extract from *Noa Noa*
1893-5

Vahine no te Vi
P Gauguin - 92

Two Tahitian Women on the Beach

1892

Honolulu Academy of Arts, gift of Mrs Charles M. Cooke 1933

Painting is the most beautiful of all the arts; in it all feelings are summed up, looking at it each one can, through his imagination, create a novel; one single glance can engulf the soul in the most profound memories, a slight effort of memory and everything is summed up instantly. A complete art that sums up all the other arts and completes them. Like music, it acts on the soul through the intermediary of the senses, harmonious hues correspond to harmonious sounds; but in painting one obtains a unity that is impossible in music, where the chords come one after the other and one's judgement is tried by an incessant fatigue if it wishes to unite the beginning and the end. Finally, hearing is an inferior sense compared to that of the eye. Hearing can only cope with one sound at a time, whereas sight embraces everything and at the same time simplifies it according to taste.

Extract from *Synthetic Notes*
1884-5

[53]

Ta Matete

1892

Oeffentliche Kunstsammlung, Basel, Kunstmuseum

Photograph: Hans Hinz

To judge a book one needs intelligence and instruction. To judge painting and music one needs something beyond intelligence and artistic knowledge, special sensations from nature; one must be, in a word, born an artist, and though many are called, few are chosen. Every idea formulates itself; it is not the same with feelings from the heart. What of efforts to master fear with a moment of inspiration; isn't love often instantaneous and almost always blind? And to say that thought calls itself spirit, while instincts, nerves, the heart are part of the material self. What an irony!

Extract from *Synthetic Notes*
1884-5

TA MATETE

Tahitian Women on the Beach

1892

The Metropolitan Museum of Art, New York

Robert Lehman Collection, 1975

But the landscape with its violent, pure colours dazzled and blinded me. I was always uncertain; I was seeking, seeking . . .

In the meantime, it was so simple to paint things as I saw them; to put without special calculation a red close to a blue. Golden figures in the brooks and on the seashore enchanted me. Why did I hesitate to put all this glory of the sun on my canvas?

Extract from *Noa Noa*
1893-5

Tahitian Landscape with a Mountain

1893

Minneapolis Institute of Arts

Julius C. Eliel Memorial Fund

I am leaving, older by two years, but twenty years younger; more *barbarian* than when I arrived, and yet much *wiser*.

Yes, indeed, the savages have taught many things to the man of an old civilisation; these ignorant men have taught him much in the art of living and happiness.

Above all, they have taught me to know myself better; they have told me the deepest truth.

Was this thy secret, thou mysterious world? O, mysterious world of all light, thou hast made a light shine within me, and I have grown in admiration of thy antique beauty, which is the immemorial youth of nature. I have become better for having understood and having loved thy human soul – a flower which has ceased to bloom and whose fragrance no one henceforth will breathe.

Extract from *Noa Noa*
1893-5

Self Portrait Wearing a Hat

1893

Musée d'Orsay, Paris

Your letter arrives at the same time as a very brief and very terrible letter from my wife. She tells me bluntly of the death of my daughter, who was taken after a few days by a pernicious pneumonia. This news did not touch me at all, long-schooled as I am in suffering: then each day, as the reflections come, the wound opens deeper and deeper and at this moment I am completely despondent. I surely have some enemy up there who does not give me a minute's rest. Whenever I start to restabilize myself with a little money to work for a few months, some exceptionally bad luck falls on me. The person who rented me a little piece of land on which to set up my hut has just died, leaving his affairs in great disorder, and as a result his land has been sold. So here I am in search of a piece of land, and I will have to build again. Besides a considerable waste of time, I estimate that it will cost me 700 to 1,000 francs; it's enough to drive you crazy. Chaudet only writes me when he has money, and I have not received anything despite what he told me before: my debt-ridden life is thus about to start up again. I received (sent by Schuff) *Les Hommes du Jour* (my absurd portrait by Schuff). That boy wears me out, exasperates me, what an idiot! and what pretence! A cross, flames, wham! there you have symbolism.

Letter to Daniel de Montfried, 1897

Nave Nave Mahana

1896

Musée des Beaux-Art, Lyons

My neighbours have become my friends. I dress like them, and partake of the same food as they. When I am not working, I share their life of indolence and joy, across which sometimes pass sudden movements of gravity.

In the evening they unite in groups at the foot of the tufted bushes which overtop the dishevelled heads of the coconut trees, or men and women, old men and children intermingle. Some are from Tahiti, others from the Tongas, and still others from the Marquesas. The dull tones of their bodies form a lovely harmony with the velvet of the foliage. From their coppery breasts trembling melodies arise, and are faintly thrown back from the wrinkled trunks of the coconut trees. They are the Tahitian songs, the *iménés*.

A woman begins. Her voice rises like the flight of a bird, and from the first note reaches even to the highest of the scale; then by strong modulations it lowers again and remounts and finally soars, the while the voices of the other women about her, so to speak, take flight in their turn, and faithfully follow and accompany her. Finally all the men in a single guttural and barbarous cry close the song in a tonic chord.

. . . More rarely, they discourse on serious questions or put forth wise proposals.

Extract from *Noa Noa*
1893-5

Where do we come from? What are we? Where are we going?

1897

Tompians Collection
Courtesy, Museum of Fine Arts, Boston

It is six metres long, two metres high. Why this measurement? Because this is the width of my studio, and I can't work without getting extremely tired at greater height. The canvas is already stretched, prepared, and smoothed out with care: not a knot, not a wrinkle, not a spot. Just think, it will be a masterpiece.

With an eye toward geometry, the composition of lines will begin in the middle, at first elliptical, then they will undulate towards the

edges. The principal figure will be a woman turning into a statue, remaining alive but becoming an idol. The figure will stand out against a group of trees like those that grow in paradise, nowhere on earth. You can see what I mean, can't you? It's not the statue of Pygmalion coming alive and becoming human, but woman becoming idol. Nor is it Lot's daughter changed into a pillar of salt: good Lord, no! From everywhere, fragrant flowers spring up; children frolic in the garden; young girls gather fruit; fruits pile up in huge baskets; in gracious postures, young and robust men carry them to the foot of the idol. The painting's appearance must be serious, like a religious evocation, melancholy, and exuberant as children.

Extract from *Diverse Choses*
1896-8

The Nightmare

1897

Courtauld Institute Galleries, London. Courtauld Collection

A young Kanaka girl is lying on her stomach, showing a part of her frightened face. She lies on a bed decorated with a blue *paréo* and a clear, chromium-yellow sheet. A violet purple background, sown with flowers like electric sparks; a rather strange figure stands next to the bed.

Seduced by a shape, a movement, I paint them with hardly any other concern than to do a nude piece. As is, the nude study is a bit indecent, nevertheless I want to make a chaste painting out of it which would render the Kanaka spirit, character, and tradition.

The *paréo* being intimately linked to the existence of a Kanaka, I use it as a bedcover. The sheet, of a fabric made from tree bark, must be yellow because when it is this colour it inspires something unexpected in the spectator, because it suggests the lighting from a lamp, which spares me having to make a lamp-light effect. I've got to have a background which is a bit frightening. Violet is everywhere. That's the musical part of the painting which has been built up.

In this rather daring position, what can a young Kanaka girl be doing completely nude on a bed? Preparing herself for love? All of this is in her character, but it's indecent and I don't want it. To sleep! The love-making still indecent, will have been finished. I see only fear. What kind of fear? Certainly not the fear of a Susanna surprised by the elders. That doesn't exist in Oceania.

Extract from *Cahier Pour Aline*
1893

NEVERMORE

Two Tahitian Women

1899

The Metropolitan Museum of Art, New York

My *vahiné*, Titi by name, accompanied me. She was of mixed English and Tahitian blood, and spoke some French. She had put on her very best dress for the journey. The *tiaré* was behind the ear; her hat of reeds was decorated above with ribbon, straw flowers, and a garniture of orange-coloured shells, and her long black hair fell loose over the shoulders. She was proud to be in a carriage, proud to be so elegant, proud to be the *vahiné* of a man whom she believed important and rich. She was really handsome, and there was nothing ridiculous in her pride, for the majestic mien is becoming to this race. In memory of its long feudal history and its endless line of powerful chiefs it retains its superb strain of pride. I knew very well that her calculating love in the eyes of Parisians would not have had much more weight than the venial complaisance of a harlot. But the amorous passion of a Maori courtesan is something quite different from the passivity of a Parisian cocotte – something very different! There is a fire in her blood, which calls forth love as its essential nourishment; which exhales it like a fatal perfume. These eyes and this mouth cannot lie. Whether calculating or not, it is always love that speaks from them...

Extract from *Noa Noa*
1893-5

And the Gold of their Bodies

1901

Musée d'Orsay, Paris

On one side [of my hut] was the sea; on the other, the mountain, a deeply fissured mountain; an enormous cleft closed by a huge mango leaning against the rocks.

Between the mountain and the sea stood my hut, made of the wood of the bourao tree. Close to the hut in which I dwelled was another, the *faré amu* (hut for eating).

It is morning.

On the sea close to the strand I see a pirogue, and in the pirogue a half-naked woman. On the shore is a man, also undressed. Beside the man is a diseased coconut tree with shrivelled leaves. It resembles a huge parrot with golden tails hanging down, and holding in his claws a huge cluster of coconuts. With a harmonious gesture the man raises a heavy axe in his two hands. It leaves above a blue impression against the silvery sky, and below a rosy incision in the dead tree, where for an inflammatory moment the ardour stored up day by day throughout the centuries will come to life again.

Extract from *Noa Noa*
1893-5

Contes Barbares

1902

Folkwang Museum
Stadt Essen

This Tahitian Eve is very subtle, very intelligent in her naïveté. Hiding in the depths of their childlike eyes, the enigma remains incommunicable for me.

It is no longer a little, pretty Rarahu listening to a beautiful romance by Pierre Loti while playing the guitar (also by pretty Pierre Loti). It is Eve after the fall, still able to walk naked without being immodest, maintaining all her animal beauty as on the first day. Her loins stay solid – maternity couldn't disfigure her: the feet of quadrumane! Fine. Like Eve, her body has retained an animal grace. But her head has progressed with evolution, thought has developed subtlety, love has imprinted an ironic smile on her lips and, naïvely, she looks into her memory for the reason for the past, for the present. Enigmatically, she looks at you.

'It's intangible,' it has been said.

Fine, I agree.

In view of the persistent physical beauty of the race, it seemed unbelievable that all its ancient grandeur, its personal and natural customs, its beliefs, and its legends had disappeared. But how was I, all by myself, to find the traces of this past if any such traces remained? How was I to recognize them without guidance? How to relight the fire the very ashes of which are scattered?

Extracts from *Noa Noa*
1893-5

Self Portrait nearing Golgotha

1896

Museu de Arte de São Paulo
Photograph: Luiz Hossaka

I have reached the age of fifty and I'm done for ... I am on the verge of suicide ... The future looks very dark to me once more, see for yourself. Still very ill, I don't know when I'll be able to work; in that case, you will receive nothing new before September 1900. From now until then, the odds are against my selling anything and in five months I will have nothing left in my pocket despite everything you have sent me. When one is late, one loses on every side. The time that I was obliged to work at the public works made me lose an enormous amount of time: I went back to find my hut in a deplorable state. The rats destroyed the roofing and as a result the rain damaged many things. A whole series of drawings, very useful records, destroyed by the cockroaches, a large unfinished canvas also destroyed by those dirty insects. I had taken my courage in both hands, and somewhat confident, reassured by your recent successes in selling, I was a little quick in forging ahead – too quick (I see it today). But it was very necessary not to lose everything, to repair the disasters, restore the roofing, and somewhat replenish my wardrobe and linen. I had *nothing* left.

Letter to Daniel de Montfried, February 1899

Self Portrait with the Yellow Christ

1889

Private Collection

Excuse the incoherence of my letter, but I am enormously agitated. This bombshell from Vollard is tormenting my brain and I can't sleep. A new doctor has come to the hospital and has taken, I don't know why, a liking to me and has undertaken to cure me, but he says it will take a long time, for the disease is very complicated and chronic. The eczema is complicated by erysipelas and by the rupture of small varicose veins.

Why didn't I die last year? I am going to be fifty-one years old, worn out, tired in all parts; my vision is becoming worse every day; so the energy necessary for this continuous struggle is running out.

Letter to Daniel de Montfried, February 1899

CHRONOLOGY

Paul Gauguin

1846-1903

1846	Born in Paris, 7 June.
1851	The Gauguin family embark for Peru, but Paul's father dies on the voyage out.
1871	Joins Paris stockbrokers' office.
1873	Marries Mette Sophie Gad from Denmark.
1874	Paints with Pissarro.
1880-6	Exhibits with the Impressionists.
1882-3	Leaves the Stock Exchange.
1886	First trip to Brittany; first ceramics. *October:* Meets Van Gogh in Arles.
1887	Travels to Panama; paints in Martinique.
1888	Second stay in Brittany; meets Serusier and Emile Bernard. Visits Van Gogh in Arles.
1889	Gauguin and his friends exhibit at the Café Volpini.

1891	Arrives in Tahiti in June.
1893	Returns to France in August. Begins first draft of *Noa Noa* and probably his first woodcuts.
1894	Finishes suite of ten woodcuts in Paris; small editions of these are printed by his friend Louis Roy.
1895	Departs for Tahiti.
1896-7	Works on *Noa Noa* and *Diverse Choses.*
1898	Attempts suicide after contemplating his major work 'Where do we come from? Who are we? Where are we Going?'.
1898-9	Begins new series of woodcuts.
1899	In June begins writing for *Les Gueppes.*
1901	In September moves to Hivaoa in the Marquesas.
1903	Dies in Atuana, Hivaoa, 8 May.

ACKNOWLEDGEMENTS

The editor and publishers would like to thank the following for their help in providing the photographs of paintings reproduced in this book:

Albright-Knox Art Gallery, Buffalo, New York (p39)
Baltimore Museum of Art (p51)
Basel Kunst Museum (p53)
Bridgeman Art Library (pp15, 47, 63)
Chrysler Art Museum, Massachusetts (p43)
Courtauld Institute Galleries, London (pp13, 67)
Essen Folkwang Museum, Stadt Essen (cover, p73)
Giraudon (p77)
Hans Hinz (pp19, 49)
Honolulu Academy of Arts (p55)
Metropolitan Museum of Art, New York (pp41, 59, 69)
Minneapolis Institute of Arts (p57)
Musée Royaux des Beaux-Arts de Belgique, Brussels (p31)
Museo de Arte de São Paulo (p75)
Museum Boymans-van Beuningen, Rotterdam (p17)
Museum of Fine Arts, Boston (p64/65)
Nasjonalgalleriet, Oslo (p23)
National Gallery of Art, Washington DC (pp7, 37)
National Gallery of Scotland. Edinburgh (pp25, 29)
National Gallery, Prague (p35)
Nelson-Atkins Museum of Art, Kansas City (p45)
NY Carlsberg Glyptotek, Copenhagen (pp9, 11, 21)
Photo RMN (frontispiece, pp60, 71)
Stedelijk Museum, Amsterdam (pp27, 33)

We would also like to thank the publishers of the following books for access to the material contained in them which has been reproduced in this volume:

Letters:
Lettres de Gauguin à Emile Bernard, 1888–91 Geneva 1954
Lettres de Gauguin à sa Femme et ses Amis Paris 1946
Lettres de Paul Gauguin à Georges Daniel de Montfried Paris 1946

Gauguin's writings:
Avant et Après Begun in 1903 and published in English with a preface by Emil Gauguin, Van Wyck Brooks, London 1921
Cahier pour Aline Begun in 1892 and edited by S. Damiron, Paris 1963
Diverse Choses Begun in 1896
Noa Noa Begun in 1893 and translated by O. F. Theis, New York 1919

Every effort has been made to contact the owners of the copyright of all the information contained in this book, but if, for any reason, any acknowledgements have been omitted, the publishers ask those concerned to contact them.